To my dearest Jeff,
Dream the great adventure.
And make it real.
Let's do it together.
You and me, forever.

I love you with my
whole ♥

Love,
Your Tricia

To my dearest Seth,
Dream the great adventure.
And make it real.
Let's do it together.
You and me, forever?

I love you with my
whole ♡

Love,
Your Tricia

What's on your top 10 list?

Acknowledgements

The quotations in this book were gathered lovingly but unscientifically over several years and/or were contributed by many friends or acquaintances. Some arrived—and survived in our files—on scraps of paper and may be imperfectly worded or attributed. To the authors, contributors, and original sources, our thanks and, where appropriate, our apologies. –The Editors

With special thanks to the entire Compendium family.

Credits:

Written and compiled by: Dan Zadra & Kobi Yamada
Designed by: Steve Potter
Edited by: M.H. Clark & Robin Lofstrom
Creative Direction by: Julie Flahiff

ISBN 978-1-935414-73-5

You're off to great places! Today is your day! Your mountain is waiting.

So...get on your way!

~Dr. Seuss

The Adventure Starts Here.

Throughout history, people have compiled lists to live by. The seven wonders of the world is a list. So are the New York Times' best sellers, the twelve steps to recovery, and the Bill of Rights.

Scientists and mathematicians have their lists. All known elements in the universe, for example, can now be conveniently listed on one page, while the list of prime numbers is thought to be infinite and never-ending.

And, of course, lovers and poets have their lists, too: "How do I love thee? Let me count the ways..."

Truth is, you've been making lists all your life: Laundry lists, grocery lists, daily to-do lists. But what about the other lists—the most important lists—the lists that shape your life, express your spirit, bring you joy, and call you to greater meaning, purpose, and adventure? That's what *10* is all about.

Set your hopes and dreams to paper, and you're halfway there!

KNOWING WHAT YOU WANT IS **THE FIRST STEP** TOWARD GETTING IT.

~Mae West

If you don't have a dream,

how can you have a dream come true?

If you haven't set goals for your life,

how can you ever hope to attain them?

Lists are an inspiring and easy way for you to

get in touch with what's really important to you,

and to visualize exciting and welcomed choices

for all the different areas of your life. Remember

that balance is beautiful. Life is a diamond with

many different facets, and you want to appreciate

them all. Why set your whole focus on money and

career, for example, if it means overlooking your

family and friends, or your creative contributions,

or your next big adventures?

There are no rules or formal directions, just this

reminder: Pick up a pen, start imagining, and have

fun. Keep your list-making fearless, spontaneous,

and real. And most important of all, don't just

make your lists—go out and do them. This is your

life—make it a great one!

...when you want something, all the universe conspires in helping you achieve it. ~Paulo Coelho

To know the road ahead, ask those coming back.

Life doesn't come with a roadmap to follow, but the closest thing is probably the inspiring Legacy Project launched by Professor Karl Pillemer of Cornell University. In 2006, he asked 1,500 older Americans who lived through extraordinary experiences and historical events to share with him their most important life lessons. Though the participants had a wide variety of knowledge and perspectives, virtually all of them chose this as one of their most important pieces of advice:

SAY YES TO LIFE AND

Say yes when things come your way. You will always regret the things you didn't do more than the things you did do.

Saying yes to life is really saying yes to yourself. "Yes" opens the door to new ideas and experiences, lets the light in, attracts kindred spirits to your journey, launches dreams and new beginnings, and spares you from later regrets. Sure, "yes" leads to change, risk, adventure, and sometimes even trouble, but "no" usually leads nowhere. Starting now, say yes to life and see where it leads you.

SEE WHERE IT LEADS YOU.

"...I AM BEHIND THE WHEEL OF MY LIFE." –DENIS WAITLEY

AT LEAST ONCE A DAY, ALLOW YOURSELF THE FREEDOM TO THINK AND DREAM.

We didn't write that headline. Albert Einstein did. He was saying: Beware of the ever-present "experts" in your life. Don't let other people tell you what or how to think. Don't let them tell you who you are, or what you can become. Whether in science or everyday life, Einstein knew the folly of accepting someone else's opinion about what's possible or factual. Those who have never run a race in their lives are happy to give you all the reasons why you can't win yours. Be your own best expert. Form the habit of saying yes to your own ideas, dreams, and aspirations. Then make lists of all the reasons why you can and will achieve them…because there will always be plenty of people around who are willing to tell you all the reasons why you can't and won't.

You
have
more
freedom

than you are using.

~Dan Attoe

ONLY ONE THING *HAS TO CHANGE FOR US* **TO KNOW HAPPINESS IN OUR LIVES:** WHERE WE FOCUS OUR ATTENTION. **THE GOOD NEWS** *IS* **THAT WE CAN CHOOSE.**

—Greg Anderson

Our time on earth is limited. We can choose to do anything, but not everything. That's why it's so important to know your priorities.

Every now and then, stop to ask yourself, "What really matters to me?"

Then ask yourself, "Am I spending my precious time on the things *that really* matter—the things I value most—or am I living someone else's dreams and *priorities for me?*"

WHAT MATTERS MOST TO ME

_____

_____

_____

_____

_____

List your top
values in order
of importance.
(For example: _____
God, family, health,
friendship, career,   _____
truth, adventure,
wealth, contribution,   _____
music.) This list
should represent   _____
your personal
priorities.   _____

NOTE: Try reading this list to yourself as an oath now and then: "I choose to live my life in alignment with my top values, and to spend my time on the things that really matter..."

What's more important…
people or things?
What's more important…
credentials or accomplishments?
What's more important…
the way you start or the way you finish?
What's more important…
where you went to school or what you learned?
What's more important…
what you acquire or what you become?
What's more important…
who people think you are or who you really are?
What's more important…
who is right or what is right?
What's more important…
your age or your attitude?
What's more important…
how you spend your money or how you spend your time?
What's more important…
what you get from life or what you give to life?
What's more important…
"say-so" or "do-so"?
What's more important…
doing things right or doing the right things?
What's more important…
how far you fall or how high you bounce?
What's more important…
making a living or making a life?

LOVE PEOPLE. USE THINGS. NOT VICE-VERSA.

~Kelly Ann Rothaus

When we die and go to heaven,

our Maker is not going to say,

why didn't you discover the

cure for such and such?

The only thing we're going

to be asked at that precious

moment is why didn't you

become you?   ~Elie Wiesel

Your past is not your **potential**

I'm learning who you've been
ain't who you've got to be...
I ain't as good as I'm gonna get
but I'm better than I used to be.

~Tim McGraw

WHAT HAVE BEEN SOME OF MY PROUDEST ACCOMPLISHMENTS?

There will always be important connections between the past, present, and future you—but you are the sum total of all you choose to become, not just all you have been.

Sometimes all we see is how far we still have to go, instead of how far we have already come. As a platform for designing your future, it's enlightening and inspiring to make a list of things you have already attempted and accomplished—the things that you are most proud of in your life. As you look over the finished list, let the positive emotions flood over you. Remember and savor how good it felt to have overcome the obstacles, and to have finally achieved those things.

Then ask yourself,

"Am I content to leave it at that?"

And, if not, start turning your gaze toward,

"Where do I go from here?"

The story of the

HOLSTEE
MANIFESTO

Manifesto/*n*/: A public and often life-changing
proclamation of intention.

Doctrines, credos, manifestos, declarations:
Down through the ages, people have compiled
words to emancipate themselves from the old
ways, and to embrace something better.

In May 2009, three young entrepreneurs—Mike,
Fabian, and Dave—decided to quit their jobs and
start a recycled clothing company called Holstee.
They knew they wanted to create eco-friendly
products that would express their passion for
life, and that they wanted to donate 10% of the
sales to other entrepreneurs in poverty-stricken
areas of the world. Beyond that, they had no
business plan, no investment capital, and no real
experience running a company.

Having just quit their jobs, they felt scared but
exhilarated about what lay before them—a feeling
they never wanted to forget. So the three of them
sat down on the steps of New York City's Union
Square and wrote down exactly what was on their
minds—not about the clothing business exactly,
but more about the new style and spirit with
which they hoped to live their lives. That way, they
might create a company that could help them put
their spirit and hopes into action. They called the
result "The Holstee Manifesto," and it eventually
found its way across the worldwide web.

It appears on the next page exactly as the three
partners scribbled it out back in 2009.

THIS IS YOUR LIFE.

DO WHAT YOU LOVE, AND DO IT OFTEN. IF YOU DON'T LIKE SOMETHING, CHANGE IT.

IF YOU DON'T LIKE YOUR JOB, QUIT.

IF YOU DON'T HAVE ENOUGH TIME, STOP WATCHING TV.

IF YOU ARE LOOKING FOR THE LOVE OF YOUR LOVE, STOP;

THEY WILL BE WAITING FOR YOU WHEN YOU START DOING THINGS YOU LOVE.

STOP OVER ANALYZING, ALL EMOTIONS ARE BEAUTIFUL. WHEN YOU EAT, APPRECIATE

LIFE IS SIMPLE. EVERY LAST BITE.

OPEN YOUR MIND, ARMS, AND HEART TO NEW THINGS AND PEOPLE, WE ARE UNITED IN OUR DIFFERENCES. ASK THE NEXT PERSON YOU SEE WHAT THEIR PASSION IS, AND SHARE YOUR INSPIRING DREAM WITH THEM.

TRAVEL OFTEN; GETTING LOST WILL HELP YOU FIND YOURSELF.

SOME OPPORTUNITIES ONLY COME ONCE, SEIZE THEM.

LIFE IS ABOUT THE PEOPLE YOU MEET, AND THE THINGS YOU CREATE WITH THEM SO GO OUT AND START CREATING.

LIFE IS SHORT. LIVE YOUR DREAM, AND WEAR YOUR PASSION.

A MANIFESTO IS A PUBLIC PROCLAMATION OF INTENTION. AND INTENTION IS WHAT BRINGS PURPOSE, MEANING, AND SIGNIFICANCE TO LIFE. THE LATIN ROOT OF "INTENTION" MEANS "TO STRETCH TOWARD SOMETHING." SO MAKE YOUR MANIFESTO A BEAUTIFUL, CRAZY, WONDERFUL "STRETCH DOCUMENT." LET IT REMIND YOU OF HOW

WRITE YOUR OWN
MANIFESTO

YOU INTEND TO EXPERIENCE AND SAVOR THE REST OF YOUR LIFE. AND WHEN YOU'RE DONE WRITING IT, FEEL FREE TO MAKE IT PUBLIC. POST IT ABOVE YOUR DESK, ON YOUR WALL, ON YOUR FACEBOOK PAGE— AND THEN LIVE UP TO IT.

THE

(your name here)

MANIFESTO

_____

_____

_____

_____

_____

_____

_____

_____

_____

_____

_____

_____

_____

_____

Dated _____

HOW WILL YOU GIVE YOUR GIFTS TO THE WORLD?

Illuminate who you are, what you might be best-suited to accomplish in the world, and how you are different from those around you by taking a personal inventory of your own talents, skills, know-how, and positive character traits.

You may need additional pages to complete your list, but the discovery is worth the work. "We are each gifted in our own special way," wrote British artist Mary Dunbar. "It is our privilege and our adventure to discover our own special light."

Once you've completed your list, stand back and ask yourself, "Which of my gifts am I actually developing and using for good—and which am I ignoring or wasting?"

We are all just skimming the surface of our true capacity. The process of actualizing our gifts and our potential is one of the most exciting and satisfying adventures of all.

Gifts and talents are what
you're born with
(natural speed, perfect pitch, etc.)

Skills are something you've developed
(martial arts, French cooking, etc.)

Education and experience are acquired
*(college degree, training, living in
a foreign land, etc.)*

Character traits are assets of the spirit
*(courage, optimism, grace under
pressure, etc.)*

talents & strengths

_____

_____

_____   _____

_____   _____

_____   _____

_____   _____

_____   _____

_____   _____

                                           _____

                                           _____

                                           _____

ANYTHING IS POSSIBLE... ANYTHING CAN BE.

~Shel Silverstein

Your third grade teacher said you had a problem with math. You gave up on math, and you forever eliminated two-thirds of the jobs available in this world.

Somebody decided the Navy needed a cook. After your hitch, you opened a restaurant. Mother was a nurse. Now you are.

Why are you where you are? Because you want to be there? Think about it. Maybe you ought to be somewhere else. Maybe it's not too late to figure out where, and how to get there.

WHY ARE YOU WHERE YOU ARE?

United Technologies Corporation ran this message in the Wall Street Journal as a non-traditional public service ad. The company received 23,060 requests for reprints and 6,157 letters from people saying that this message had inspired them to evaluate their life's work and make a change.

HOT ON THE TRAIL OF YOUR TRUE CALLING

The place God calls you to is the place where your deep gladness and the world's deep hunger meet.

~Frederick Buechner

Throughout life, there's a voice that only you can hear, calling you to do your real work in the world. If you hear it and heed it, then your work will become one of your greatest joys.

A JOB is just a task you do to pay the bills.

A CAREER is primarily motivated by titles, notoriety, or advancement.

A TRUE CALLING is doing exactly what you love most—your passion—and knowing that you will be appreciated and rewarded for it, both now and at the end of your life.

You don't have to climb a mountain in Tibet to search your soul for your true calling. You can actually discover it by simply identifying your greatest joy or your most persistent yearning.

MOVING TOWARD MY TRUE CALLING

Step 1: Write your Purpose Statement in the space below.

In general, what is the primary joy that you seek to express in your life and work? Your answer doesn't need to be profound; it needs to express your most persistent yearning or interest. Chances are you already know the answer, even if it's vague: "musical expression," or "caring for the less fortunate," or "working with kids," or "traveling the world," or "teaching and empowering others," or "preserving nature" or "political activism."

My Purpose Statement

Step 2: List several ways you might express your Purpose Statement as an actual vocation.

Make a list of ten areas that you might be interested in working in. Then narrow it down by circling your top 2-3. For example, if your purpose statement is "preserving nature," and your top areas of interest are "writing," "working with endangered animals," and "environmental activism," chances are your true calling and dream job are likely to be found in one of those three, or in combination.

_____   _____

_____   _____

_____   _____

_____   _____

_____   _____

If your dreams were a place, a place,

where would you be standing, and what would you be looking at?

In your wildest dreams...

Dreams are the picture-making power of your imagination. They are the stuff of which life, hope, love, fun, adventure, and accomplishment are made. Respect and nurture your dreams—believe in them—and bring them into the sunshine and light.

It's been said that there isn't one person in a thousand who can write down their most exciting dreams and aspirations, without telling themselves all the reasons why those dreams and aspirations can't happen: It's too difficult, too expensive, too impractical, never been done before, not feasible—why bother?

The big question of, "Why aren't I living my dreams?" can usually be answered simply: You either haven't written your dreams down or, if you have, you may have already started to talk yourself out of them. You can change that right now by starting your master dreamlist.

> You must go
> after your wish.
> As soon as you
> start to pursue
> a dream, your
> life wakes up
> and everything
> has meaning.
>
> ~Barbara Sher

my
dreamlist

_____

_____

_____

_____

_____

_____

_____

_____

Suggestions:

- Turn on some inspiring music.

- Quiet the negative voices.

- Write down some of your most cherished dreams. Anything goes! Graduating from Juilliard? Buying a 200-acre horse ranch in Montana? Starting an e-business, and selling it for $100 million in five years? It's your dream, so write it down.

- Try to include one dream for each of your earlier "What Really Matters to Me" list.

- Don't worry about prioritizing your dreams yet; just let them flow.

Once you've written your dreamlist, and written down your values, you're on your way. The next step is to convert your dreams into goals, and then your goals into action plans. "Dreams are fun to talk about," says Anthony Robbins, "but when dreams are turned into goals, they become possible. And when goals are turned into plans, they become real."

A dream without a goal is just a wish

YOUR PERSONAL GOAL-SETTING GUIDE

BALANCED: SET GOALS FOR ALL AREAS OF YOUR LIFE, NOT JUST ONE OR TWO. USE YOUR VALUES AS A GUIDE. **PRIORITIZED:** YOU CAN DO ANYTHING, BUT YOU CAN'T DO EVERYTHING ALL AT ONCE. FOCUS FIRST ON YOUR MOST IMPORTANT DREAMS AND GOALS. **POSITIVE:** INSTEAD OF, "I DON'T WANT TO BE OUT OF SHAPE ANYMORE," BE POSITIVE: "I WILL ACHIEVE THE IDEAL WEIGHT FOR MY HEIGHT."

SPECIFIC: INSTEAD OF, "I WILL OWN MY OWN BUSINESS," BE SPECIFIC: "I WILL OPEN AN OUTDOOR GUIDE SERVICE IN THE TETON MOUNTAINS." **MEASURABLE:** HOW WILL YOU KNOW WHEN YOU'VE REACHED YOUR GOAL? INSTEAD OF, "I WANT TO BE A GOOD DISTANCE RUNNER," TRY: "I WILL RUN A MARATHON IN UNDER FOUR HOURS."

VALUABLE: FOCUS ON THE "WHY." KNOW ALL THE REASONS WHY THIS GOAL IS PERSONALLY VALUABLE AND IMPORTANT TO YOU. **ACHIEVABLE:** SET GOALS THAT ARE CHALLENGING AND CURRENTLY OUT OF REACH, BUT POSSIBLE TO ACHIEVE.

TIME-BOUND: GOALS ARE DREAMS WITH DEADLINES, SO SET SCHEDULES. WITHOUT A SCHEDULE, SOME GOALS MIGHT TAKE FOREVER TO ACCOMPLISH. **RECORDED:** KEEP YOUR GOALS SOMEPLACE VISIBLE. REVIEW AND AFFIRM THEM AT LEAST 2-3 TIMES EACH WEEK. **UPDATED REGULARLY:** KEEP DREAMING, GROWING, LEARNING, DARING—

AND SET NEW GOALS ACCORDINGLY.

ACTION IS ELOQUENCE...

~WILLIAM SHAKESPEARE

DREAMS DON'T COME
TRUE BY THEMSELVES.
GOALS AREN'T ACHIEVED
BY ACCIDENT.
PLANNING IS THE
"HOW" OF YOUR LIFE—
AND IT DOESN'T
HAVE TO BE DIFFICULT.

Nothing happens without an action plan.

TURN THE PAGE,
AND YOU'LL DISCOVER
A SIMPLE BUT EFFECTIVE
ACTION PLAN—A WAY
TO MOVE YOURSELF
FROM DREAM TO GOAL
TO ACTION TO COMPLETION.

A SAMPLE PLAN OF ACTION

Write down one goal from your dreamlist:

Example: Climb Mt. Fuji in Japan.

What excites me about this goal?

Because it's there, and it's a climbable mountain for an amateur. I think it would be a great personal challenge, and a great way to get in shape. Besides, I've always wanted to see Japan.

What are the obstacles that I can control that keep me from moving forward?

I don't know how to get started. I'm not in shape, and I don't have enough money for the trip. Plus, I'd need to take time off from work.

What are the solutions to the obstacles?

Search online for "Climb Mt Fuji" for info on joining a climb, and join a hiking club to get in shape. Get a weekend job to earn extra money, and request an extra 10 days off next summer for the climb.

Go back to the goal and rewrite it as if it has already happened for you:

I feel proud and exhilarated as I look out across the Japanese countryside from the summit of Mt. Fuji. It feels great to be in the best climbing shape of my life, and I can't wait to tour the Japanese countryside after I descend.

MY PERSONAL PLAN OF ACTION

1) One goal I have selected from my dreamlist:

_____

_____

_____

2) What's in it for me? What excites me about this goal?

_____

_____

_____

3) What are the obstacles that I control that keep me from moving forward?

_____

_____

_____

4) What are the solutions to the obstacles?

_____

_____

_____

5) My goal restated as if it has already happened for me:

_____

_____

_____

Planning is bringing the future into the present so that you can do something about it now. ~Alan Lakein

1 my life one year from now:

_____

_____

_____

_____

The future turns out to be something that you make instead of find…

It isn't…any further away than the next sentence, the next best guess, the next sketch for the painting of a life portrait that might become a masterpiece.

The future is an empty canvas or a blank sheet of paper, and if you have the courage of your own thought and your own observation, you can make of it what you will.

~Lewis Lapham

10

Visualize life's coming attractions.

Standing on top of your life, what do you see?

Think of your vision as your ideal picture. Think of your goals and action plans as your step-by-step commitment to that ideal.

5 my life five years from now:

_____

_____

_____

_____

_____

my life ten years from now:

_____

_____

_____

_____

_____

20 my life twenty years from now:

_____

_____

_____

_____

_____

What do you stand for?

IT WAS AN INTERESTING SHOWDOWN. WHEN THE CONSERVATIVE OLD J.C. PENNEY COMPANY, INC. ANNOUNCED THAT ELLEN DEGENERES WOULD BE THEIR NEW SPOKESPERSON, THOUSANDS OF PEOPLE THREATENED TO BOYCOTT THE STORE. AFTER ALL, THEY SAID, ELLEN IS GAY—AND A GAY PERSON SHOULDN'T BE ALLOWED TO REPRESENT SUCH AN ICONIC AMERICAN COMPANY. SURELY, JCPENNEY WOULD SUBMIT TO THE PRESSURE. INSTEAD, COMPANY CEO RON JOHNSON SPOKE UP WITH THIS STATEMENT: "WE STAND SQUARELY BEHIND ELLEN AS OUR SPOKESPERSON. JCPENNEY WAS FOUNDED 110 YEARS AGO ON THE GOLDEN RULE, WHICH IS ABOUT TREATING PEOPLE JUST LIKE YOU WOULD LIKE TO BE TREATED YOURSELF. AND WE THINK ELLEN REPRESENTS THE VALUES OF OUR COMPANY." IN THANKING JCPENNEY AND OTHERS WHO RALLIED TO SUPPORT HER, DEGENERES DECIDED TO DEFINE HER OWN VALUES: "I WANT TO BE CLEAR...I STAND FOR HONESTY, EQUALITY, KINDNESS, COMPASSION, TREATING PEOPLE THE WAY YOU WANT TO BE TREATED, AND HELPING PEOPLE IN NEED." END OF CONTROVERSY. YOU COUNT. YOU MAKE A DIFFERENCE. SILENCE IS AN OPINION. STAND UP AND SPEAK UP FOR SOMETHING OR SOMEONE EVERY DAY. MARTIN LUTHER KING SAID, "OUR LIVES BEGIN TO END THE DAY WE BECOME SILENT ABOUT THINGS THAT MATTER." JOURNALIST MARY WALDRIP PUT IT THIS WAY: "IT'S IMPORTANT FOR PEOPLE TO KNOW WHAT YOU STAND FOR. IT'S EQUALLY IMPORTANT FOR THEM TO KNOW WHAT YOU WON'T STAND FOR." NOW'S YOUR CHANCE.

Things I stand for...
(TRUTH, COMPASSION, FREEDOM, FAIRNESS, ETC.)

Things I won't stand for...
(MEAN PEOPLE, BIGOTRY, POLLUTION, CRUELTY TO ANIMALS, ETC.)

Clarify your principles.

...keep the rebel artist alive in you ~Norman Mailer

You were a kid once, full of hope, curiosity, and creative rebellion. Your imagination knew no boundaries. You made up stories, and pretended. You broke the rules here and there, and you colored outside the lines. You marveled at just about everything, and you felt seduced—seduced to have fun, to take a dare, to wander and wonder, to question the way things have always been done, to yearn and to learn, and to seek new quests and half-crazy adventures. What happened?

"Routine parches the artist," writes Jennifer Louden. "If there is one cosmic law I know the consequences of ignoring, it is this one: You cannot create from an empty well. Your creative center, the place where the artist resides, must be fed. She must go spelunking in crystal caves, gorge herself on gory fairy tales, sip 1908 vintage port and curse like a sailor, sleep in a 300 year old white pine tree, exult like 103 year old potter Beatrice Wood, and imbibe succulent art and fresh perspective for breakfast, lunch, and dinner."

...break away from routines

BE
FEAR

...we lean forward to the next crazy venture beneath the skies. ~Jack Kerouac I've been thinking a lot lately about taking chances, and how it's really just about overcoming your fears. Because the truth is, every time you take a big risk in your life, no matter how it ends up, you're always glad you took it. ~JD Scrubs Anything in my life that was ultimately worthwhile… initially scared me to death. ~Betty Bender Take into account that great love and great achievements involve great risk. ~Dalai Lama Every great idea that changed the world came from someone who was brave enough to call for it. ~Sylvia Boorstein I learned to embrace risk, as long as it was well thought out, and, in a worst-case scenario, I'd still land on my feet. ~Eli Broad To live is not about breathing, it is about action. ~Jean-Jacques Rousseau No matter what we feel or know, no matter what our potential gifts or talents, only action brings them to life. ~Dan Millman What you risk reveals what you value. ~Jeanette Winterson Things won are done; joy's soul lies in the doing. ~William Shakespeare We do not need magic to transform our world. We carry all the power we need inside ourselves already… ~J.K. Rowling I looked outside myself for strength and confidence, but it comes from within. It was there inside me, all the time. ~Anna Freud Living is a form of not being sure, not knowing what next or how…We guess. We may be wrong, but we take leap after leap in the dark. ~Agnes de Mille Courage can't see around corners, but goes around them anyway. ~Mignon McLaughlin …to the degree we are lost, it is on the same ocean, in the same night. ~Elizabeth Kaye If you wait for the perfect moment when all is safe and assured, it may never arrive. ~Maurice Chevalier This is my life. It is my one time to be me. I want to experience every good thing. ~Maya Angelou If you do nothing unexpected, nothing unexpected happens. ~Fay Weldon Accept what life offers you and try to drink from every cup. All wines should be tasted; some should only be sipped, but with others, drink the whole bottle. ~Paulo Coehlo I don't always know where I'm going, but I have promised myself that it won't be boring. ~Unknown

LESS

Never turn your back on your own ideas.

Guglielmo Marconi was a foolish dreamer. Marconi was born in Bologna, Italy in 1874. At school, he read about Leonardo Da Vinci's soaring imagination. Back in the 1500s Da Vinci had made impossible sketches of eyeglasses, airplanes, and helicopters. He did it by indulging in foolish flights of fancy—something he called his "fantasia."

Inspired, young Marconi did some imagineering of his own. When he was just 20, he created a clunky wireless device in his father's basement that could transmit radio signals. His father thought he was lying, but when young Marconi convinced him there were no wires, his father emptied his wallet right on the spot for more supplies.

Next, Marconi wrote to the Italian ministry, explaining his wireless telegraph machine, and asking for funding. Ridiculous! The Minister laughed, and said Marconi should be sent to the Lungara Asylum in Rome. Marconi thought about quitting. Instead, he built a bigger, crazier machine, dragged it outside the basement, and proved he could transmit a military signal over a hill 1.5 miles away. No one laughed this time.

Soon, Marconi was known as the Father of Modern Radio. He won the Nobel Prize and became a hero on a scale that Italy hadn't seen since Da Vinci. When the Titanic sank in 1912, the world credited Marconi with saving 705 lives. Why? Because the Titanic's modern radio was able to call in rescue ships at night.

Despite his celebrity, Marconi worked long into each night on his next crazy-beautiful idea. Even in his 60s, after four heart attacks, he refused to slow down or give up. And what an idea it was! In a recent PRX Public Radio segment, narrator Nate DiMeo described it this way:

Marconi became convinced that sound never dies—that sound waves, once emitted from a radio, or from the vibrating strings of a Stradivarius, or from whispering lovers… that those sounds get weaker but live on forever. We just hadn't built a radio powerful enough to recapture the signals.

So here was Marconi near the end of his life, growing weaker with each heart attack, dreaming of a device that would let all of us tap into these eternal frequencies. He wanted us to be able to hear everything…hear Jesus of Nazareth giving the sermon on the mount…hear Caesar's voice, hear Shakespeare giving an actor a line…hear someone tell you they loved you that very first time. Hear everything. Forever.

Marconi might have been wrong about that idea. Or maybe, like Da Vinci, he was just ahead of his time. Either way, he was willing to play the fool on our behalf. He not only thought of that impossibly beautiful idea, but he went after it with his last breath.

You, too, have a creative contribution to make. Something small, something big, something utterly fantastic or foolish—an idea unique to you—your fantasia. Never turn your back on your own ideas. You may not live to see all of them realized, but be as foolish as Marconi and chase them anyway. The world will be better if you do.

Ask, "What if?"

Those two little words can open new worlds for all of us, in every facet of work, love, and life.

After Apple CEO Steve Jobs died, his friend John Lasseter recalled that part of Steve's genius rose from constantly and courageously asking himself, "What if?"

"No one likes their cell phone," Jobs once told Lasseter, "so what if I make a phone that people love?"

"What if you could have a thousand songs in that little phone in your pocket?"

"What if you could store a thousand photos on it?"

"What if you could easily edit your own home movies right there on your phone?"

Make yourself a promise: Pick up a pencil, now and then, and ask yourself "What if?" Just think of something that would be really wonderful if it were only possible, and write it down on your "what-if" list. Then see where your ideas take you.

My "what-ifs"

Jot down ten of your most hopeful, courageous, or outrageous "what-ifs"—
and then ask yourself, **"Why not?"**

what-if

what-if

what-if

what-if

what-if

what-if

what-if

what-if

what-if

what-if

"Why not?"

Martin Luther King, Jr. called these
six little words the most persistent
and urgent question of all:

What are you doing for others?

Roll that question over in your
mind, and answer it thoughtfully,
knowing that the most certain
way to bring hope, help, meaning,
and joy to your own life is by
bringing hope, help, meaning,
and joy to the lives of others.

WHAT AM I DOING FOR OTHERS?

Ways I am reaching
out, serving, helping,
inspiring, teaching,
mentoring, or comforting
those around me.

_____

_____

_____

_____

_____

_____

_____

_____

_____

The greatest
thing is,
at any moment,
to be willing
to give up
who we are
in order
to become all
that we can be.
~Max De Pree

In an episode of the TV sitcom "30 Rock," CEO Jack Donaghy (Alec Baldwin) hallucinates that he has met up with his future self. Mr. Future gives Jack some great advice that helps him avoid major mistakes in life. True to Jack's character, of course, most of the advice has to do with things he should probably STOP doing.

It's true for all of us. You can have any life you choose, but in order to have the things you really want, you must be willing to stop doing the things that are holding you back.

Having filled out the lists in this book, you may now find it easier to say no to the people, habits, or excuses that have been holding you back. It's always easier to say no when you have a bigger and better YES to look forward to.

My Old No's   My New Yes's

things to do before I die

A "bucket list" is a compilation of all the interesting things you want to do before you kick the bucket. Everyone has a bucket list inside them, but not everyone has taken the time to write it down. Creating the actual list is an exciting step, because it increases the chances that you will actually check those items off as you make them happen. Bucket lists are usually quirkier or more adventurous than, say, a list of your top ten lifetime goals. A typical bucket list item might be something like this pearl from writer Sean Fogle: "Go to Cuba before the embargo is lifted, and enjoy a great cigar." In February 2012, Fogle successfully crossed that one off his list, but you can add it to your list if you want. There are no penalties for copying someone else's bucket list. In fact, if you search "bucket list," you'll find literally thousands of ideas that other adventurous souls have posted online.

LIVE IN A TREE-TOP TENT FOR A WEEK IN THE AMAZON JUNGLE

HERE ARE SOME OTHER EXAMPLES TO STIR YOUR CREATIVE JUICES:

VISIT EVERY MAJOR LEAGUE BASEBALL STADIUM ✺ SING THE STAR SPANGLED BANNER AT A SOLD-OUT EVENT ✺ DRINK CHAMPAGNE AT AL CAPONE'S OLD BAR IN CHICAGO ✺ FIND MY ANCESTRY ✺ SEE THE NORTHERN LIGHTS ✺ BACK-PACK THROUGH EUROPE ✺ LEARN JAPANESE ✺ RUN A MARATHON ✺ DONATE 20 GALLONS OF BLOOD ✺ FLY IN A FIGHTER JET ✺ JAM WITH MOSE ALLISON ✺ RECORD AN ALBUM OF ORIGINAL SONGS ✺ READ THE 100 GREATEST NOVELS ✺ VISIT A MUSIC FESTIVAL IN ALL 50 STATES ✺ CREATE A NON-PROFIT ORGANIZATION ✺ SHAKE HANDS WITH THE PRESIDENT ✺ GO INTO SPACE ON VIRGIN GALACTIC ✺ BE AN EXTRA IN A HOLLYWOOD MOVIE ✺ LEARN TO SAIL A 40-FOOT SAIL BOAT ✺ WALK TO THE TOP OF THE EIFFEL TOWER ✺ TAKE A COOKING CLASS IN FLORENCE, ITALY ✺ FIND AN AMAZING MENTOR ✺ WATCH ROGER EBERT'S TOP 102 MOVIES OF ALL TIME ✺ SEE A GIRAFFE IN THE WILD ✺ PLAY A ROUND OF GOLF AT AUGUSTA NATIONAL

GO EVERY-WHERE. LIVE EVERY-THING.

MY BUCKET LIST:

Tip: Think of this as a work in progress—something you can add to all the days of your life. Start with a few items today, and whenever you think of something new, just add it to your bucket.

HOW DO YOU ADD MORE LIFE TO LIFE?

TIME IS A GIFT YOU GIVE YOURSELF

What kind of mountains could you move if you suddenly had two or three more hours of time added to each day? One way to find out is to simply identify and eliminate your top time-wasters. Do that, say social scientists, and you'll redeem an average of three hours each day to spend on the hopes, dreams, people, and projects that are most important to you—that's 80,000 hours over the course of a lifetime.

Everyone has their own list, but some of the top time-wasters that are easiest to correct are a cluttered desk, a poor filing system, constantly checking e-mails, watching TV, and the inability to say no to friends or co-workers.

Time is too short and too wonderful to squander. You are here on earth for a reason. Say yes to the things and people you should say yes to, and say no to the things and people that waste your time, or that take advantage of your big heart.

MY TOP TIME-WASTERS
Pick three to eliminate right away:

What will tomorrow bring?
You get to decide.

Lots of people get up in the morning and live out their day, then they go home at night and think about what happened and how they feel about it.

Tonight, try something different. Just before your head hits the pillow, visualize the kind of day you want to have for yourself when you wake up. Not just the routine things, but also a few audacious surprises. Turn the list over to your subconscious and sleep on it, knowing that whatever you've imagined for tomorrow can and probably will happen.

If you like what happens the first day, continue your new nightly routine for a week or two. By then, you will definitely have something new to think about.

With our thoughts, we make the world.

-Siddhartha Gautama

There are two kinds of check lists.

One is a regular "to-do" list with little empty boxes next to each item. Checking off your to-do list is a satisfying way to celebrate another day checking off all the things you chose to complete. You can find this kind of to-do form at any office supply store, or even find one online.

The second kind of list—the "ta-da" list—is even more satisfying. It's an inspiring and magical list of reminders about what you strive to include in each day of your life, no matter what, no matter what, no matter what.

Here are some examples of a ta-da list:

Did I wake up and greet the day?
Did I celebrate just being alive?
Did I read something interesting today?
Did I find at least one piece of good news?
Did I learn something new?
Did I change something for the better?
Did I think about my future?
Did I stop to thank someone?
Did I put something—even just a dollar—in savings?
Did I find something to make me laugh?
Did I make someone else laugh?
Did I help or reach out to someone?
Did I forgive someone (maybe even myself)?
Did I do something sacred (pray, meditate, visit the sick)?
Did I stand up for someone or something?
Did I do something ridiculous or fun?
Did I tell my loved one(s) how much I appreciate them?
Did I treat my body well?
Did I write down at least one new idea?
Did I take a chance on something?
Did I review my most important lifetime goals?
Did I count my blessings?

Imagine how good you'll feel if you can say "Ta-da!" to these kind of questions at the end of each day.

My daily ta-da list

Add to the world's

joy.

Ring in the New!

Keep growing, changing, and improving.

In the 1940s and 1950s, a folk singer from Okemah, Oklahoma challenged the way Americans thought about culture and society, using nothing but his voice, an old guitar, and some occasional stick figure drawings.

Woody Guthrie composed more than 3,000 songs and poems, drew more than 500 illustrations, and wrote three books, always reminding us that life is made up of little things. He believed that everything and everyone counts, that there is no such thing as an insignificant person, neighbor, or intention—and that small changes are still vital changes.

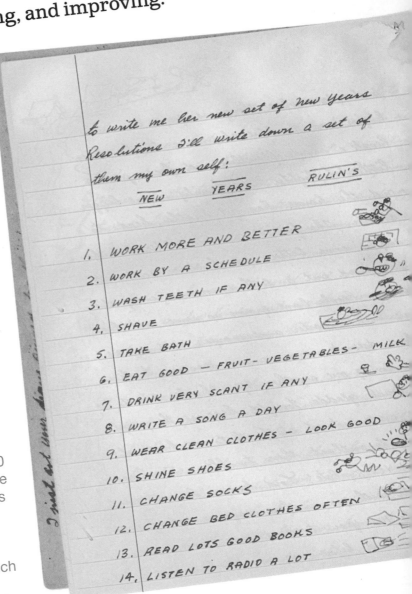

to write me her new set of new years
Resolutions I'll write down a set of
them my own self:

NEW   YEARS   RULIN'S

1. WORK MORE AND BETTER
2. WORK BY A SCHEDULE
3. WASH TEETH IF ANY
4. SHAVE
5. TAKE BATH
6. EAT GOOD — FRUIT — VEGETABLES — MILK
7. DRINK VERY SCANT IF ANY
8. WRITE A SONG A DAY
9. WEAR CLEAN CLOTHES — LOOK GOOD
10. SHINE SHOES
11. CHANGE SOCKS
12. CHANGE BED CLOTHES OFTEN
13. READ LOTS GOOD BOOKS
14. LISTEN TO RADIO A LOT

One of his most beloved pieces is this hand-drawn list of New Year's Resolutions, plucked right from his journal. Like all good resolutions, Guthrie's "Rulin's" are simple and sensible, but adopting a few of them could actually change the world for the better.

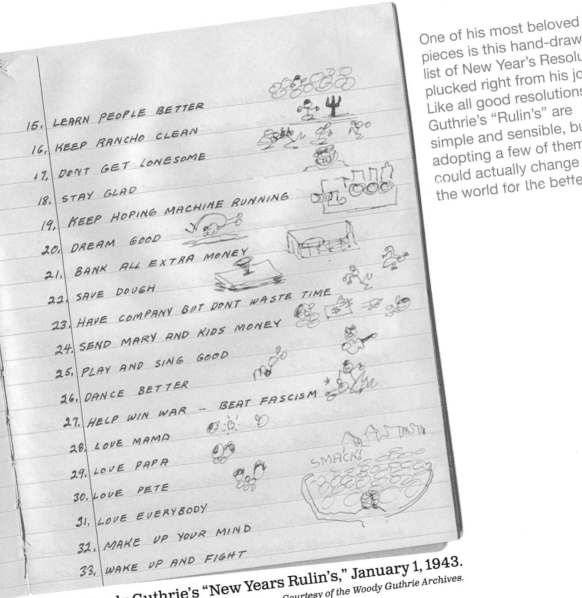

15. LEARN PEOPLE BETTER

16. KEEP RANCHO CLEAN

17. DONT GET LONESOME

18. STAY GLAD

19. KEEP HOPING MACHINE RUNNING

20. DREAM GOOD

21. BANK ALL EXTRA MONEY

22. SAVE DOUGH

23. HAVE COMPANY BUT DONT WASTE TIME

24. SEND MARY AND KIDS MONEY

25. PLAY AND SING GOOD

26. DANCE BETTER

27. HELP WIN WAR — BEAT FASCISM

28. LOVE MAMA

29. LOVE PAPA

30. LOVE PETE

31. LOVE EVERYBODY

32. MAKE UP YOUR MIND

33. WAKE UP AND FIGHT

Woody Guthrie's "New Years Rulin's," January 1, 1943.
Courtesy of the Woody Guthrie Archives.

Who knows why it's so hard, even in the closest relationships, to say what needs to be said before it's too late?

~Karl Pillemer,
The Legacy Project

When the Legacy Project interviewed 1,500 older people near the end of their lives, the most grateful were those who had managed to say what needed to be said while they were still young, or while there was still time—even if it was just a simple "Thank you," or "I love you."

One of the Legacy respondents, Ruth Helm, tragically lost her college-age daughter in a plane crash and spoke for all the other respondents when she said, "One thing we always did, whenever we would get off the phone we always said, 'I love you.' And I was so happy that we did that because when I said good-bye to my daughter, the last words that I said to her were 'I love you.'"

"For some regrets," continued Ruth, "there are possibilities for do-overs and second chances. Leaving critical things unsaid or unasked, however…can't be changed after the person is gone. If you have something to say to someone, say it now."

....

....

....

....

....

People I will contact, speak to, or thank...now instead of later.

....

....

....

....

....

LIFE IS AN EXCITING, EVER-CHANGING BANQUET OF NEW EXPERIENCES AND POSSIBILITIES TO SAVOR, BUT ONLY IF YOU MAKE IT SO. REGULARLY REVISIT, REFRESH, AND RENEW YOUR MOST IMPORTANT LIFELISTS—AND CONSTANTLY BRANCH OUT INTO NEW LISTS AND NEW FRONTIERS TO EXPLORE.

DON'T STOP HERE— MAKE YOUR OWN TOP 10 LISTS

IF YOU'RE LOOKING FOR FRESH IDEAS, YOU'LL FIND LOTS OF KINDRED SPIRITS ON THE WEB WHO ARE WILLING TO SHARE LIST IDEAS WITH YOU. SOME ARE SERIOUS, SOME ARE QUIRKY, SOME ARE CEREBRAL, SOME ARE SPIRITUAL, SOME ARE SENTIMENTAL, AND SOME ARE JUST PURE ADVENTURE AND FUN. HERE IS A CROSS-SECTION TO GET YOU STARTED:

WHAT GIVES ME HOPE FOR THE FUTURE? • WHO OR WHAT HAVE I FORSAKEN? WHO ARE THE CHILDHOOD FRIENDS I WANT TO RECONNECT WITH? • WHAT ARE THE THINGS I LOVE MOST ABOUT MY WORK? • WHICH THINGS WILL I NO LONGER PROCRASTINATE ABOUT? • WHAT ARE THE SIMPLE PLEASURES I WOULD LIKE TO MAKE MORE TIME FOR? • WHICH FAMILY TRADITIONS DO I WANT TO KEEP, AND MAKE EVEN MORE MEANINGFUL? • WHAT PLACES IN MY OWN CITY DO I WANT TO EXPLORE? • WHAT THINGS DO I WANT TO TRY FOR THE FIRST TIME? • WHO ARE THE HAPPIEST PEOPLE I KNOW, AND WHY? • WHAT CAN I DO TO GIVE MYSELF MORE PEACE OF MIND? • WHAT ARE SOME WAYS I AM COMMITTED TO BEING HEALTHIER? WHAT ARE SOME THINGS I WOULD LIKE TO DO WITH (OR FOR) MY FRIENDS? • WHAT ARE SOME SPECIFIC WAYS I CAN EXPRESS MY LOVE FOR MY FAMILY? • WHAT ARE SOME THINGS I'D LIKE TO ASK MY FATHER AND MOTHER? • WHAT ARE THE 10 BEST PIECES OF ADVICE I HAVE EVER BEEN GIVEN? • WHAT DO I LOVE BEST ABOUT MY LIFE? • WHEN WERE THE TIMES IN MY LIFE WHEN I FELT MOST ALIVE? • WHICH FAMILY RECIPES SHOULD BE WRITTEN DOWN AND PASSED ON WITH LOVE? • WHAT ARE SOME OF MY MOST VALUABLE THINGS THAT MONEY CAN'T BUY? • WHO ARE THE ANCESTORS I WANT TO KNOW MORE ABOUT? • WHAT ARE THE STRESSFUL THINGS IN MY LIFE THAT I PLAN TO DO SOMETHING ABOUT? • WHAT ARE SOME WAYS I WILL LESSEN MY IMPACT ON THE PLANET? • WHO ARE THE PEOPLE AND/OR POTENTIAL FRIENDS I WOULD MOST LIKE TO MEET? • WHO ARE THE PEOPLE WHO HAVE MOVED AWAY THAT I WOULD LIKE TO CONTACT? • WHAT ARE THE THINGS I WOULD DO IF I SUDDENLY LOST EVERYTHING? • WHICH THINGS SHOULD I DONATE OR GET RID OF BECAUSE THEY ARE JUST COLLECTING DUST? • WHAT ARE THE THINGS I WILL DO NOW TO ENSURE A FUN AND MEANINGFUL OLD AGE?

my lists

Care deeply. Create opportunities. Make something good happen.

Be passionate. Begin anywhere. Attempt the untried. Get carried away. See for yourself.

my list

Make someone's day. Stay in touch. Settle for more. Be inspired by what you do not know. Try something new. Give back. Make a difference.

my lists

Pursue your dreams. Raise your expectations. Be spontaneous.

Start a new tradition. Embrace big ideas. Make every moment count. Enjoy your life.

Don't just make your lists—go out and live them.